The Geometry of Distance

First Published in the UK in 2012 by Mantle Arts

Copyright © Katie Daniels, 2012

The right of Katie Daniels to be identified as author of this work have been asserted by her.

This book is sold subject to the condition that it shall not, by the way of trade or otherwise, be lent, resold, hired out, or otherwise circulated without the publisher's prior consent in any form of binding or cover other than that in which it is published and without a similar condition, including this condition, being imposed on the subsequent purchaser.

ISBN 978-0-951504055

Mantle Arts
Springboard Centre
Mantle Lane
Coalville
LE67 3DW
www.mantlearts.org.uk

Printed and bound in the UK by Imprint Digital,
Upton Pyne, Exeter, EX5 5HY

Cover illustration by Louise Scott
www.louise-scott.co.uk

The Geometry of Distance

Katie Daniels

For Brian, of course

and for my brother, Chris
(to whom I apologise for failing to include
the lost penguin at Copacabana.
I hope he found his way home.)

Think of the long trip home.
Should we have stayed at home and thought of here?
Where should we be today?

Elizabeth Bishop – Questions of Travel

Contents

Leicestershire: March, April, May, June

Strongroom, Wigston Record Office	8
This drug	9
Codebreaking	11
Freefall	12
This marriage is over	14

Brazil: July

Departures	16
First view of São Paulo	18
On the balcony, first night in Brazil	20
Wedding	21
São Paulo vignettes	22
O Cristo Redentor	24
Restaurant, Rio de Janeiro	25
On the mountain, Petropolis	26
We cross the Tropic of Capricorn	27
Boat, Paraty	29

Church of Santo Antônio, Tiradentes	31
Airport	32

Near and Far

Crossing the rope bridge with your son	35
Red balloon	36
Griffin	37

Leicestershire:

March, April, May, June

Strongroom, Wigston Record Office

Feels like skin, I say as I reach down
a manuscript from the shelf. A piece of hair
falls across the locket at my throat
and you see what's gone before roll aside,
turning into wills and inventories.
I step back too quickly, treading on toes,
and you tell me, though we've never met before,
that nothing is sustainable - yet in this
height and silence and cool grey air
we can't get away from what lasts.
This manuscript of skin I touch is bound
with cord I'm too apprehensive to untie
so I run my fingers along the shelves, searching
for the familiar, but it's tightly packed, and won't come loose.

This drug

I

This drug is   the one that switches off
                    my pituitary gland,
                    terminating hormone production.

This drug is   the one that stimulates
                    my egg follicles
                    into swelling fronds.

This drug is   too high a dose:
                    sends my overblown ovaries into overdrive,
                    causing treatment to be abandoned.

This drug is   unspoken: an Adoption Information Evening
                    and a silent dinner
                    with my husband afterwards.

II
This drug is   acceptance.
              It is never going to happen.

III
This drug is   fantasy: two hours in a strongroom
              with a stranger
              have begun to unravel me.

This drug is   truth: heady enough
              to tell you, who I barely know,
              that your email brought me joy.

This drug is   the grape and the grain
              you drink before you reply
              Be reassured.

This drug is   the cocktail of chance
              I reach for
              as the other drugs cave in.

Codebreaking

The radio plays music from a film score
as I drive down the street with flowering cherry trees
and the wind brings tiny pink blossom rushing
towards me
                up and over the car,
tripping like soda under my tongue.
                                      Later it rains
and you and I find shelter where the sky drips
from the blue steel of a fire escape.
You kiss my neck and we are codebreakers
finding paths and patterns, sitemaps,
tagging one another's skin, your day
and mine as though the two could be anything
but disparate.
                                We write it together
with fingers and tongues, soft places, drifting
into May with galleries and crypts
of sleeplessness pulling us on.
                                We sanction this
curatorship - you give me
an autograph book with histories
that aren't mine to decipher;
I give you codewords, questions flowering,
blown towards us fast as spring.

Freefall

You walk across the car park with your shirt off.
It's June, and the planes
of your not yet familiar chest surprise me.
A whole afternoon, a whole evening ahead,
laying with you in wet bracken,
watching the tiny movements under your eyelids,
the slight curve of your tender mouth,
while the batteries playing us *Songdog* run down.

You said you fell in love that day.
You went down on me in the rain.
Later in a stranger's driveway
I lifted my head from you
and reached for red wine;
saw green avenues of rain on glass,
felt my skirt fall about my thighs
as I picked up the cup.

This summer slips us through – odd hours
and afternoons with you, from one
to the next, like falling from a cliff:
each hour a jutting ledge, a tree.
Letting you and the day go
means hard minutes of freefall;
my hands holding the empty space
that held you a moment before.

This marriage is over

As my husband's wedding ring hits the window sill
my ears are still taking in the sound
of *This marriage is over*, although I know it is.
You're having an affair – the cumbersome truth
that unravelled somehow. Unseen lives slip:
I watch it disappearing, that elusive child,
our frozen embryos, our one miscarried foetus, gone.
Brazil's four weeks away. He never really wanted
to go. *I want you out of this house*
tomorrow is the deadline he gives me.
He leaves his wedding ring lying where it fell.

He leaves his wedding ring lying where it fell.
Tomorrow is the deadline he gives me
to go. *I want you out of this house.*
Brazil's four weeks away. He never really wanted
our frozen embryos, our one miscarried foetus, gone.
I watch it disappearing, that elusive child
that unravelled somehow. Unseen lives slip:
You're having an affair. The cumbersome truth
of this marriage is over. Although I know it is,
my ears are still taking in the sound
as my husband's wedding ring hits the window sill.

Brazil:

July

Departures

Just the one person travelling?

Yeah.

                (What a fuck-up.)

Terminal 2:
here comes my big adventure,
past this neon pink light box,
through door H

where three lads with Brummie accents
get louder when I sit down.

                (Yesterday you were a stranger again
                in your blue shirt,
                your features becoming new
                even before *goodbye*.)

I've a bag full of tobacco for my brother
and I'm thirsty as hell. I watch
a Sikh in a black turban
comfort his father in a red one.

> (This is an interlude
> in the journey, in us;
> a pause before moving forward again.)

Arrivals
is the other side of the world.

First view of São Paulo

The Sahara was seven hours ago.

        (Long haul: in it for the.
        Are we?)

This is a first:
Southern hemisphere,
new territories,

        (my hand on the skin of your abdomen,
        yesterday)

new oceans and deserts
laid open below me.

In two days, my brother
will marry a girl
I've met only once.

        (Just geography, this distance
        that you recede into.)

Her city on the flight screens:
layer on layer of civilisation
unfolds like patchwork beneath me,

unveiling *city*
on implausible scale.

What I thought was the city
was just a glimpse of the city.

Now the flight screens are peeling off
quilt after quilt.

On the balcony, first night in Brazil

Yellow three quarter moon lies low –
one amber crescent missing from the top –
over the favela's climbing road.
The moon appears to be the wrong way up,
suspended with me from an overturned earth.
Streetlit traffic noise coaxes me down
to where smoke in the dark of my brother's breath
tempts me across a balcony of sound.
The sheer scale of this sideways moon;
one telling lightless curve that folds
to empty like a journey done
where the hillside is too steep to build –
stark hole in the favela's net of lights.
I crave one of my brother's cigarettes.

Wedding

Today is my birthday; I'm thirty-five years old. I open my presents in the van on the way to the wedding.
It's midwinter and hot. Nanda arrives very late; she is stunning. I am to be a Padrinha, which is like a bridesmaid; but they only come in couples. I don't have a Padrinho. The Brazilians become anxious. My Uncle Malcolm steps in. Afterwards we eat; the food is churrasco[1] and good. Nanda's sleazy cousin tries to get into my pants. I slip off for a fag with my brother; we sit on a flight of steps leading nowhere, looking out over a gully of green. I keep checking my phone, but there's nothing. The Brazilian wedding singer begins a Beatles medley; out of context, all wrong. The Brazilians bring a birthday cake for me. Everyone sings. I join my brother on the dance floor for two, maybe three songs, giving it my all. It makes Nanda smile. Later, at a bad hotel, I download emails to my phone; there are four from you, but none say 'happy birthday'. This is because you have the wrong date; you think it's tomorrow. It is tomorrow, where you are. Tomorrow we'll drive back to São Paulo, sit in eight lanes of traffic in surreal midwinter heat. This was the wedding; this was why we came.

---

[1] Churrasco: Brazilian cooking style translating roughly from the Portuguese for 'barbecue'.

São Paulo vignettes

1. The day after her wedding
my brother's wife
breaks a mirror
while unloading the van.

2. My brother carries her
over their threshold. I say
She ain't heavy, she's my sister.
Nanda says she loves me.

3. From their balcony
we look down on boys and chickens
playing kickabout
on the bright pink earth.

4. We go for a walk.
I see a white dog
with astonishing blue eyes
in a city I find surprisingly green.

5. You send me an email. It says
how much you miss your mum
and that she would have loved me.
I feel lonely all day.

6. My mother says *Take care of yourself darling*
but she's so far from what I need.
Precarious, and so low key: no pity.
We are in fragile territory.

O Cristo Redentor

This was
the pinnacle
of temptation
(the biblical kind)

now here's redemption:

Christ the Redeemer stands 39.6 metres tall at the peak of the Corcovado [2] mountain

spiny earth curves
with the weight of it

two gulls cling
to the folds of His robe

two semicircles carved
into His taut open palms

stone corrugates
about His feet

construction
took nine years

here, where
redemption
was carved
from temptation

I look up
into Christ's empty eyes

---

[2] The mountain was originally given the biblical name 'Pinaculo da Tentacao' (Pinnacle of Temptation) by the early Portuguese, but its name was later changed to Corcovado because of its resemblance to a hunchback.

Restaurant, Rio de Janeiro

This restaurant is for the rich.
At the meat counter fish counter fruit counter
stainless steel and marble chillers and platters
brim and spill over, empty and are refilled.
Suspended from the roof is a miniature railway.
A tiny train provides constant backbeat:
chucka chucka chucka chucka.

The main course is churrasco.
'All you can eat'.
I ask for beef first
but it is rare, much too rare for me.
It falls wetly to my plate.
I watch my rice turn slowly pink.
Blood drips onto the tablecloth.

At my end of the table
they are speaking Portuguese.
In the absence of the language,
my appetite & you, I think how much
your son would love the train
moving above our heads. A waiter takes away
my plate of untouched bloody meat and rice.

On the mountain, Petropolis

We met an armadillo
on the sharply rising track to the hotel.
My brother stopped the van to let it pass,
slow and scaly. The track is so steep
that the van slipped backwards, and Bernardo,
from the hotel, helped push us to the top.

(The route you take is the armadillo:
I cannot rush it. I can't make you walk
until you're ready, even if it means
backsliding, disembarking for a while, getting help.)

Here, at an altitude of one thousand metres,
a blind kitten appeared during the World Cup.
They called him Corner Kick.
He curled in my warm lap last night
as I spoke to you in another hemisphere
from Bernardo's pc in the hotel office.

At night I'm alone in a seven foot wide bed.
Meanwhile I'm taking comfort where I can:
embracing that black dog on the mountain today,
just to have something, anything, to hold.

We cross the Tropic of Capricorn

where the sun turns back at the solstice,
hemispheres tilting. This noon
we watch a roadside vendor
strip the bark from sugarcane,
mill it to juice, add lemon.

In our hired van, my brother, my new sister-in-law,
my parents, my aunt and uncle and I
drive to the coast. No-one mentions

my fallen-down marriage, my absent
soon-to-be-ex-husband; the empty seat
filling up with bottles of water,
my mum's jacket, my dad's camcorder.
No one mentions you, but I have pictures:
Inter-railing, gloriously tall;
footballing, holding your son.
Decades of you I'll never know.

Peel it back - it's tough as fibres;
through the mill, crushed and sweeter,
stripped of our known constellations,
we step over some universal line.
I want you there when I fold sheets;
dance; sleep; laugh. But tonight
I'll drink *Caipirinha*[3] until my eyes hurt,
walk cobbled streets in the warm winter dark.

---

[3] Brazil's national cocktail, made with Cachaça, sugar and lime. Cachaça is an alcoholic drink made through the fermentation of sugarcane juice.

Boat, Paraty

> Oh God! If there was a paradise on earth, it would not be very far from here! *Amerigo Vespucci on Paraty*

On the yellow roof of our hired boat
the day rises - through the boat's blue floor,
through its sunwarm roof
into the skin of my legs,
into blood and bone;
ocean fizzing with sunlight
at the back of my eyes.

The town recedes, we dive in:

silver fish with yellow stripes
brush against my body as I dive;
thoughts of you are bright stripes
as I swim, gentle ocean dipping
in hidden places,
fish brushing my arms and legs,
skimming past my back, my shoulders.

We find islands, we are docking:

a man with a snorkel walks out of the ocean
holding a starfish a foot wide.
Later we drift,
turning off the boat's engine,
drifting in the boat with the yellow roof;
supple grey leaping all around
where I stand still and look look look:

my eyes fill up with dolphins.

Church of Santo Antônio, Tiradentes

For Barbara
1931-2006

Inside, God's house is full of gold
with numbered floorboards.

This was your mum's birthday.
Beneath a dark Madonna

I greet somebody I never knew:
Your son, I say. *He's really something.*

Outside, a hummingbird
is a small black signature on a white wall.

Some saint of spurious miracles
clocks this shadowed, iridescent tag

of pure movement in silhouette:
an absence of light, beating.

Airport

At check in
I have to explain again
that there is only one of me,

going home to

        (what home?
        Twenty packing boxes stacked in the hall.
        A rental contract that isn't valid
        for another two weeks.

        You're in Amsterdam
        with your partner and kids,
        one last family holiday.
        I've seen the looks my friends give -
        He won't go through with it
        is what they're thinking

        but
        I
        believe
        in)
the unknown.

My aunt puts her arm around me
and walks with me towards passport control.

Near and Far

Crossing the rope bridge with your son

You're watching us on the climbing frame
as we stop at the rope bridge.
You say *You'd best carry him*

    so I pick up your son for the first time

                                      - warm two year old -

    and we step onto the bridge,

                        clutching the rail

    my sandaled feet

                        uncertain

    on shifting ground,

                        surfaces blurring,

across wooden slats weaved into red rope. Precarious –
the routes we take – but over this unsteady ground
we sense you walking, somewhere alongside.

Red balloon

I am holding a red balloon with long silver string.
This is the baby I lost.
I want to let it go.
I am on the boat near Paraty
because I am happy here. Everything is still.
The red balloon is still, but every week
I let the silver string slip
a little further through my fingers.

Maybe next week I will let it go.
This week
the soft frayed end of the silver string
lays against the tip of my index finger.

I can come here whenever I like.
The red balloon with the silver string
will be here, still hovering
above the still ocean.
No-one knows about the red balloon
or the boat that brings me here

or how it feels when the last fibre
of silver string
slips
from my open hand.

Griffin

I
Meet me by the pond;

sit here, on this fallen tree.
Tell me it's love.

Smooth grey wings rock me.
Some unseen shutter falls.

I wandered round the same dead space
only to find this within myself:

loving somebody
more than me.

II
My brother in a phone box,
trying to write my number
with a burnt match head;

smoke curls past the family hair.

There's a cheap big view
of a far-off city
under the cloak
of what shapes him:

the geometry of distance.

Wear it like a chain.

Acknowledgements

The Geometry of Distance was written with the support of a National Lottery grant from Arts Council England (Grants for the Arts) for writing time.

Thanks are also due to Harborough District Council for an Arts Development Grant towards mentoring costs, and to Aoife Mannix for her sensitive and constructive mentoring.